A
Rookie
reader

To Grandmother's House We Go

Written by Charnan Simon
Illustrated by Mernie Gallagher-Cole

Children's Press®
A Division of Scholastic Inc.
New York • Toronto • London • Auckland • Sydney
Mexico City • New Delhi • Hong Kong
Danbury, Connecticut

For my mom and dad, grandparents extraordinaire.
—C. S.

To Me Me and Pa. two terrific grandparents.
—M. G. C.

Reading Consultant

Cecilia Minden-Cupp, PhD
Former Director of the Language and Literacy Program
Harvard Graduate School of Education
Cambridge, Massachusetts

Cover design: The Design Lab
Interior design: Herman Adler

Library of Congress Cataloging-in-Publication Data

Simon, Charnan.
  To Grandmother's house we go / written by Charnan Simon ; illustrated by Mernie Gallagher-Cole.
      p. cm. — (A rookie reader)
  Summary: Simple text about a family visit provides an introduction to prepositional phrases.
  ISBN-10: 0-531-12089-9 (lib. bdg.)   0-531-12491-6 (pbk.)
  ISBN-13: 978-0-531-12089-7 (lib. bdg.)   978-0-531-12491-8 (pbk.)
  [1. Air travel—Fiction. 2. Grandmothers—Fiction. 3. English language—Prepositions—Fiction.] I. Gallagher-Cole, Mernie, ill. II. Title. III. Series.
  PZ7.S6035To 2006
  [E]—dc22   2006006761

Mom always sings the same song when we visit Grandma.

To Grandmother's house

But the song is wrong!

WE get in a taxi when
we go to Grandma's house.

We drive to the airport.

the sleigh....

We walk through the sliding doors.

We stand in line to
check our bags.

It seems that we go

We ride on the moving
sidewalk to get to our gate.

Straight through the

We get on the airplane.

We take off!

When we land, we wait for our luggage.

We get in ANOTHER taxi.

I see Grandma!

I love going to Grandma's house!

**Maybe Mom's song is
not wrong after all!**

Yum!

Word List (95 words)

(Words in **bold** are prepositions.)

a	fast	I	our	stand
after	**for**	**in**	**over**	straight
airplane	full	is	pie	take
airport	fun	it	play	taxi
all	gate	knows	pumpkin	that
always	get	land	ride	the
and	go	line	river	**through**
another	going	love	same	**to**
bags	grandma	luggage	see	trot
barnyard	grandma's	maybe	seems	visit
but	grandmother's	mom	sidewalk	wait
cap	gray	mom's	sings	walk
check	ground	moving	sleigh	way
dapple	guide	my	sliding	we
day	hard	not	slow	when
doors	have	now	snow	white
dreadful	horse	**of**	so	woods
drifting	house	**off**	song	wrong
drive	hurrah	**on**	spy	yum

About the Author

Charnan Simon lives in Madison, Wisconsin, but she wrote this book at the picnic table in her parents' backyard in Walla Walla, Washington. Her kids are mostly grown now, but when they were little they loved taking family vacations to visit grandparents in Walla Walla and Chicago!

About the Illustrator

Mernie Gallagher-Cole draws and paints pictures from her home in Pennsylvania. Her kids, Glenna and Ian, are adored by their grandparents.